We Older People

We Older People

WANDA MARIA BÜHRIG

JUDSON PRESS
Valley Forge

WE OLDER PEOPLE

This book was originally published in German under the title, *Erfulltes Alter,* © 1963 by Christliches Verlagshaus, Bern. English Translation © The Saint Andrew Press 1969.

Translated by Kathleen M. S. Easton

Judson Press Edition 1971

International Standard Book No. 0-8170-0500-5
Library of Congress Catalog Card No. 77-124992

Printed in the U.S.A.

Foreword

In this little book a few thoughts on old age are gathered together. An old person speaks to her contemporaries and seeks to share some of her experiences with them.

It is not easy to write about old age, because this period of life cannot be viewed objectively, since one cannot proceed beyond it. Youth and the years of maturity pass, and one can look back upon them, but not upon old age. One is encompassed by one's old age, and it is brought to a close only by death, which seals the lips forever. Before that, there often comes a period of twilight, in which it is no longer possible to survey one's past years logically. For this reason my thoughts should be regarded as the fruits of my journey through all the stages of life.

They are, however, not intended solely for old people, but also as a help for those who are middle-aged and feel they have to come to terms with old age, or who view old age with apprehension, perhaps because they have trouble with old people. This little book seeks to awaken in such people sympathy for the problems of old age and to show them that old age can be a time of serenity. As such a preparation for old age, my thoughts will merely act as a stimulus; they do not seek to instruct, but to encourage independent meditation.

I hope that this work of mine will be of comfort, especially through the fifty texts quoted in it. They have been selected at random. I trust readers will themselves choose others from the riches of Scripture, ones which have a special message for them and which will help them to make of old age a time of satisfied fulfillment.

WANDA MARIA BUHRIG

Zurich

The life which I now live in the flesh I live by the faith of the Son of God, who loved me, and gave himself for me (Galatians 2:20).

When we reach a certain age, the question sooner or later occupies us: Am I still alive? Is it still living, to shuffle along like this, or to hear and see badly, and to be thrust more and more firmly out of the community of one's fellow-creatures? Of course one knows objectively that one is alive, but subjectively it is a burning painful question. At this point we older people are challenged by the words: "The life which I now live in the flesh. . . ."

This can be applied to any physical situation; the life I still live in hobbling along, in pain, with failing memory, I nevertheless "live by the faith of the Son of God." Suddenly our life ceases to be aimless; we see its goal pointing us to eternity.

What awaits us there? The love of Christ, "who loved me, and gave himself for me."

But we really have to live with such words—not just read them once and then quickly forget them with our failing memories—every day and every sleepless night, until they really spring to life.

For ye serve the Lord Christ (Colossians 3:24).

"Serve" was a word spoken to slaves, to men who toiled hard doing uncongenial compulsory work.

But what has that to do with us? Have we older people not been thrust out of the activity of work; are our little daily tasks worth mentioning; can we honestly still be of service?

There is no mention here of tasks completed, just simply of service! The knitting I still do, the supper I get ready, the letter I write, the flowers I look after, the prayer I offer. Service? Yes, it can all be service, even the slightest everyday occurrence. Only we must understand the word "serve" correctly. It is not *de*serving; it is simply serving the Lord Jesus Christ.

What he makes of our service is his business. Slaves often did not know the purpose of their work and were obliged to suffer the whims of their masters. We have a Master who rules the world, even within our four walls, and we know his unchangeable love.

And when we are at the end of our strength, completely dependent on the help of others, then more than ever are we in service. That is in the difficult service which is the struggle with our impatience and intolerance. And we can always pray, even if only in heartfelt sighing. Prayer is divine service.

So teach us to number our days, that we may apply our hearts unto wisdom (Psalm 90:12).

Does our present life acquire more value and color if we dwell upon death? It is true that something within me desires the end. Every occurrence, every period of life, every encounter must have an end. That is why the final stage of a piece of work, even if it be only some needlework, is something really gratifying.

But, on the other hand, life is sweet, and the thought of death fills us with dread. One does not desire the end, often not even when life has become very hard.

Luther's translation of this text from the Psalms runs: "Teach us to remember that we are mortal, so that we may attain wisdom," and this we can attain when we survey our lives in the light of our mortality. How? By being afraid and trying to run away from death? No, indeed—by seeing in each day which is vouchsafed to us a gift of great price; by valuing our todays, living them and using them to the full. For life in this world is not everlasting, and the final stage is death. The wise are they who do not fritter away their lives but use them in God's service.

Today if ye will hear his voice . . . (Psalm 95:7) .

The voice of God calls us today. But is an old person's "today" not often sheer misery? Is it then not better to forget "today," benumb my senses with radio or television, or give myself up to useless complaining?

Or shall I deem every hour important because it is transient and maybe even offers the last chance to do something? Today I can still do things as I wish. But tomorrow, or in a month, or in a year? How many paths are already closed to me in the literal and the figurative sense? And the great dread may lay hold on me, dread of illness, of pain, of dependence, of disability.

Yet do we know what tomorrow will bring? Have we not often found that the future turns out to be quite different from what we have hoped or feared?

Therefore we must learn, if we have not yet done so, that life, even yet in old age, must be centered on "today." For today is a gift from God, and the future is composed solely of todays. Today his voice calls us, *if we will hear it!* Let us strain our ears to listen, even at sad and difficult times, but above all let us not forget it in all the moments of brightness which we meet on our way.

Then Abraham gave up the ghost, and died in a good old age, an old man, and full of years (Genesis 25:8).

When we search the Old Testament for sayings on old age, we soon notice that in those days old age was not a "problem" but one of God's blessings. Ripe old age is a reward. "There shall not be an old man in thine house" (1 Samuel 2:31) is meant as a penalty.

At the same time the Bible speaks in all moderation of old age; it does not gloss it over but sees clearly all the disadvantages and infirmities of age.

Yet a ripe old age is a "good" age, and the satiety with life which is often spoken of indicates not that one is tired of life but that one is satisfied with a life fully lived.

Such an old age is something to look forward to. Then no one need — as so often happens now because people will not make the most of old age — attempt a long and mostly unsuccessful escape into an imaginary youthfulness.

At evening time it shall be light (Zechariah 14:7).

This passage speaks of an old age of satisfaction, an old age in the light! It is a wish for us all, whatever age we have reached.

Of course our text does not refer to old age. The prophet Zechariah is describing the coming of the kingdom of God. Nevertheless, the text has a message for us, too, if we look on the light as the light of God, which can and should shine on the eventide of every life and transfigure old age, even if we do not always perceive it. Clouds obscure the earthly light of the sun, but it is our faults, moods, and weaknesses which obscure the heavenly light. The sun shines in spite of the clouds, for if it did not, all life on earth would perish. All the more does the light of God shine ceaselessly. Were it otherwise we should be lost to all eternity.

"At evening time" — our eventide, too — "it shall be light." But we must believe in the light, the light of God, which has revealed itself in Jesus Christ to us.

Even to your old age I will be the same,
when you are grey-haired, still I will sustain you;
I have borne the burden, I will carry it,
yes, I will carry you and save you.
(Isaiah 46:4, Moffatt)

Why are we so easily inclined to lose heart and to surrender to the gloomy view of life, especially of being and of growing old? Perhaps because we rely on ourselves and forget Him who bears us up with his strength.

"When you are grey-haired." So we readily accept the gray hairs, for we know that when God is sustaining us, life is worth living. Thus old age, too, can be a time of satisfied, nay, of joyous fulfillment. But we must not expect joy to come of its own accord and only when we are old. Old age is prepared for in youth.

A comment from the early nineteenth century (Burdach, quoted by Dr. Vischer) contains an excellent truth. "But when in early life nothing lasting has been achieved, old age admittedly lacks substance."

It is unreasonable to expect youth to look ahead to its old age. It is youth's business to prepare for its life, its occupation, and its service in the world. But those in middle years might well do so. For example, when the first signs of age appear (as soon as one has to emphasize one's youthfulness, one no longer possesses it!), it is undoubtedly high time to think of one's spiritual state. We do so by recognizing who sustains us when we are gray-haired and who will continue to carry and save us. We must make room for Him in our lives to acknowledge and gratefully accept this power.

And as thy days so shall thy strength be (Deuteronomy 33:25).

This is what we fear at the first signs of dwindling strength – the complete disappearance of our powers, the dependence on others.

The blessing of Moses upon one of the tribes of Israel promises its members strength to the end of their lives. "Thine age shall be as thy youth," the text runs in Luther's translation.

This could be a part of our prayer and supplication! At any rate, let us consider such a state as a possibility.

Whether it will be vouchsafed to us personally we do not know, but alongside the familiar image of the helpless graybeard this other one can present itself, the image of the man who although failing in physical strength is blessed with divine strength to the last.

"Cast me not off in the time of old age; forsake me not when my strength faileth" (Psalm 71:9). Can we ourselves help here? Yes, by not weakening too soon, nor being sorry for ourselves and taking it easy. For one can either try to be too youthful or, on the other hand, be too ready to enjoy the ease of old age. The right strength comes from God. "Forsake me not," prays the psalmist, and we join in his prayer.

PROSPICE

Fear death? – to feel the fog in my throat,
  The mist in my face,
When the snows begin, and the blasts denote
  I am nearing the place,
The power of the night, the press of the storm,
  The post of the foe;
Where he stands, the Arch Fear in a visible form,
  Yet the strong man must go:
For the journey is done and the summit attained,
  And the barriers fall,
Though a battle's to fight ere the guerdon be gained,
  The reward of it all.
I was ever a fighter, so – one fight more,
  The best and the last!
I would hate that death bandaged my eyes, and forebore,
  And bade me creep past.
No! let me taste the whole of it, fare like my peers
  The heroes of old,
Bear the brunt, in a minute pay glad life's arrears
  Of pain, darkness and cold.
For sudden the worst turns the best to the brave,
  The black minute's at end,
And the elements' rage, the fiend-voices that rave,
  Shall dwindle, shall blend,
Shall change, shall become first a peace out of pain,
  Then a light, then thy breast,
O thou soul of my soul! I shall clasp thee again,
  And with God be the rest!

Robert Browning

Forsake me not, O God, when I am old and grey;
that I may tell the rising generation
of thy strength and thy might (Psalm 71:18, Moffatt).

The greatest difficulties of old people are caused by their feeling cut off from society, which I suppose is unavoidable because it is an essential feature of old age. The younger generation is often unjustly accused of being the cause of this. That may be so in isolated cases of especial heartlessness, but not always. One's own generation dies out, and so isolation automatically occurs.

Thus arises the plea in our text: "When I am old"—precisely then—"forsake me not." When one is aware of this help and this presence, solitude—hard though it may be to begin with—becomes more and more animated, more attractive.

The psalmist knows what is needed—he entreats for himself a task—that of making God known to the next generation. One knows from experience how often it is the grandmothers who make God real to their grandchildren.

To the old, one can say: "Learn to be alone, in the active solitude of your old age, secure in the presence and help of God, and be ever on the alert to notice a task waiting for you."

In returning and rest shall ye be saved; in quietness and in confidence shall be your strength (Isaiah 30: 15).

In old age we often have quite enough of rest and quietness, so that instead of bearing us up they get us down.

Nonetheless it is the task of old age to switch from doing to being, which many people find very difficult. Conscious *being,* actually more important than *doing,* is hard to attain in the dynamics of everyday life and cannot be attained easily in old age either, because anything which one could not do before will certainly prove difficult later on. Tranquillity needs to be learned. Here it must be noted that tranquillity and inaction are not the same thing. On the contrary, tranquillity is something extraordinarily active, a suffusion with life, which comes from God, and we know how, on the other hand, inaction, lack of something to do, can be tedious.

The so-called primitive peoples know more about this than we do. Thus one description of a primitive youth states: "He does not require to kill time; he sits quietly down and lives."

And we? We seek ways of passing the time, because time is not important enough, although in old age especially it should be. Old age can be a time of grace in which one can learn real tranquillity, the tranquillity which brings us salvation and strength.

Even the youths shall faint and be weary, and the young men shall utterly fall: But they that wait upon the Lord shall renew their strength; they shall mount up with wings as eagles; they shall run, and not be weary; and they shall walk, and not faint (Isaiah 40: 30-31).

Shuffling feebly along the streets leaning on our canes, we find it difficult to believe in these promises. Perhaps we are not trusting enough in the Lord, we think, and resolve to try harder.

That certainly will do us no good, for this message is one of grace and not of effort or reward. But when we grasp it, we notice that even those incapacitated by age constantly receive new strength, even if it does not manifest itself physically. It can be bestowed anywhere it is needed. Are our earthly ploys then so important for the Lord's work? Scarcely.

We would understand better the meaning of what Isaiah says if we read the whole of the fortieth chapter, whose closing words form this text. Eagles' wings and strength to walk are promised to those who fulfill God's commands. Many Jews who were transported to Palestine from their primitive homelands in airplanes, never having seen such a thing in their lives before, saw the eagles' wings of God in these technical structures; for they waited upon the Lord and were looking for the coming of his kingdom.

Strength is not the monopoly of a particular time of life, for "youths shall faint and grow weary." Even the old can acquire pinions! Let us believe this in order to attain strength.

If a man live many years, let him have joy throughout them all; let him remember that the dark days will be many (Ecclesiastes 11:8, Moffatt).

Yes, the days of darkness, the hours of dread, of sadness, of anxiety — "they will be many." It seems simple to take pleasure in the easy days. But it is not always so. Have we not many a time spoiled a good day by bad humor or plain discontent? Are we not guilty of this very frequently when old?

Granted there are often trifles, such as being uneasy or off color, which prevent full enjoyment, but it is partly our business to see the good side in spite of them.

And the days of darkness? When we think of them in retrospect, we do not need to gloss them over. They were hard, even if subsequently we recognized God's guidance in them.

And the present days? Could we not learn to be grateful for them? For even the dark hours, the sleeplessness, and the pain are part of life, this full, beautiful, and blessed life given by God!

They shall still bring forth fruit in old age; they shall be fat and flourishing; to shew that the Lord is upright: he is my rock, and there is no unrighteousness in him (Psalm 92:14-15).

"It is a good thing to give thanks unto the Lord, and to sing praises unto thy name, O most High: To shew forth thy lovingkindness in the morning, and thy faithfulness every night." So begins the psalm whose closing verse is above.

Is it not the desire of the old still to bear fruit and their greatest grief to be useless and, so to speak, thrown on the scrap heap? Now they have the promise that they can bear fruit, fat and flourishing.

What is the prerequisite? Living with God, not only all of a sudden when one is old and banished into one's room, but from one's youth up; for unless one has already learned and proved this, one can scarcely bear fruit in the evening of life, although with God all things are possible.

So the old person, who has perhaps been late in learning to give praise, should not neglect to do it. How nice it is to meet an old person who speaks the praise of God, the praise of the lovingkindness and faithfulness which he has received all his days! It is good to follow God's ways throughout life; then much will be filled with new vigor, difficulties will be accepted, happiness will be more radiant, the incomprehensible will acquire meaning.

Let your weaklings think them[selves] warriors, let your cowards think them[selves] heroes! (Joel 3:10, Moffatt). *Let the weak say: I am a hero* (Zurich Bible).

Has this text a message for us old people? The prophet Joel is actually dealing with the assembling at the last day when the call to judgment rings out, when courage is all needed, so that the challenge to heroism, that is, to be strong, becomes obvious.

But has this text any message for us in our far from heroic daily life? I am sure it has, for it is a challenge to do our best. We are so often fainthearted, peevish, of little faith. We are sick of everything, and we do not know what we are here for unless to have a nice comfortable easy time. We are the weaklings!

Now our text bids us exhort ourselves: I am a hero; that is, I should strive with all my might not to let myself go, not to think of my ease, but to wait and see what God wants of me.

What is a hero? Even heroes are afraid. But they are the ones who in spite of fear and human weakness are prepared to fling themselves wholly into the fray. They are not heroes by nature; they become so by bringing their being into line with God's.

Neither does Joel appeal to the strong but to the weak like us. So he has a word for us and spurs us on to heroism in everyday life and to readiness quietly to devote our powers where it is required of us. There is plenty of heroism in old age, particularly when illness sets in and death approaches.

So may we all become heroes!

Have nothing to do with those godless myths, fit only for old women. Keep yourself in training for the practice of religion (1 Timothy 4:7, NEB) .

These are words which hurt many an old woman because she sees in them contempt for her age and sex. But that is not necessarily the case. There are in the Bible many women of advanced age who command respect.

In olden days there were, and even yet are, in the villages old women who pass on ancient lore, a mixture of medical knowledge and superstition, of local custom and pagan usage. Such lore cannot hold its own in the clear light of the gospel. But familiarity with such "godless" lore is without doubt closely linked with old age, for it presupposes a certain amount of experience.

The author of the letter to Timothy is no doubt chiefly protesting against the pagan and the superstitious in such traditions, to which old people, especially women, are susceptible, the more so because in old age one often loses the ability to discriminate.

A lot that we valued in the "good old days" of our youth falls into the category of such fables. Let us learn to distinguish, and try to shake off our preferences and judge impartially. Instead of collecting "fables" and clinging obstinately to ancient tradition just because it is ancient (there is, of course, some worth keeping!) , let us hold fast to the Bible. There, instead of fables, we find God's word and his truth.

For the word of God is alive and active (Hebrews 4: 12, NEB) .

Fortunate are we that in old age we have time to read the Bible. When work presses, there is often little time for that. But what is to prevent us older people from living with the Word?

Unfortunately all sorts of things prevent us if we have not become familiar with the Bible earlier on. Even the Book of Books can be uncommunicative, for one cannot learn overnight how to deal with the living Word. Nevertheless, the Word is alive for elderly inexperienced readers, too, if they seek an approach to it, and there are countless people who by reason of being old know the Bible better than younger ones, whose time is overfilled with worldly matters. Of course Bible knowledge is not peculiar to any age group, but it may be a privilege of old age to have more time to become at home with it.

It is a good preparation for old age to have known the Bible earlier and to learn from it how to employ one's time.

"The word of God is alive and active." No other book in the world can take the Bible's place, for the Bible really is living and has a personal message for the reader. Those who in youth, perhaps with much sighing, learned Bible texts, bless this knowledge in their old age. For suddenly even the imperfect memory of age brings treasures of the Word to the surface to strengthen them and quicken them.

The days of our years are threescore years and ten; and if by reason of strength they be fourscore years, yet is their strength labour and sorrow (Psalm 90:10).

Well, this is perhaps a grand subject for lamentation! One could pity oneself or even secretly preen oneself for having borne this hard life so well!

The psalmist is simply making a statement lest we become proud of our lives and look back thinking all our past good and fine, eventually believing in the myth of the "good old days" that never were. Then of course we were young, capable of achievement and enthusiasm—but then, as now, much was good and much was bad.

It is not easy to find the right way to view the past, to see it in its true light as transitory, as Psalm 90 points out, contemplating what was good without too much hankering after past days and what was hard without bitterness or reproaches. The outcome of our excursion into the past will be the test—does it make us sad, despondent, peevish, or do we feel deep gratitude for all our experiences?

It is not given to every old person to bind life into a resplendent bouquet of memories. How many sins of omission and commission there are in every life! But we can always trace God's guidance throughout our past, and how good it is to appreciate this guidance in the many trifling details of existence!

Cast me not away from thy presence; and take not thy holy spirit from me (Psalm 51:11).

Ah, that ancient misdeed again! A blush still comes to our aged cheeks when we remember many an incident in our lives. How could I? But I did! And of ourselves we can efface nothing from our lives, take not a word back, and only in exceptional cases can we redress a wrong. "Too late" stands menacingly over us as we look back. It is a good thing to recognize our guilt; then we will not gild our past. Nor can we say loudly or softly every time our neighbor lapses, "*I* would *never* have done that!"

We must not, however, remain entangled in our transgressions. We bring them with the psalmist before God and entreat his forgiveness — "Take not thy holy spirit from us." For that is the worst thing about sin; it shuts us off from the companionship of the Holy Spirit and estranges us from God, though we are better off than the people of the Old Testament, knowing as we do of the forgiveness which Jesus Christ has won for us by his death. Let us hold fast to this forgiveness.

If we confess our sins, he is faithful and just to forgive us our sins, and to cleanse us from all unrighteousness (1 John 1:9).

It is necessary to review the past to realize our sins and to confess them before him, not trying to gloss over them and explain them away. But we need not stop in the past, for Jesus Christ is "faithful and just" and forgives us our sins.

Cleansed from all unrighteousness by his mercy, we look back. What we see is lit up, and the past sends a beam of light into the present. We relive the "pleasant times" from our youth up to our old age, and our survey gives us pleasure and fresh courage.

For it is not good to dwell upon our misdeeds. Gratefully we accept forgiveness for them, to be free in the service of the Lord Jesus Christ, who is no respecter of age but calls all to follow him.

Peace be with you! (John 20:19, NEB).

A sentence I once read in a newspaper arrested my attention: "In these harassing days oases of peace are especially necessary. And old people are better fitted to create these than anyone else."

That would indeed be a task worth living for—to be oases of peace!

But are we able? Certainly Jesus often addresses us as he does his disciples, with this greeting, but we are stubborn. No one can spread peace, be an oasis of peace, who has not peace in his heart, and humanly speaking it is not a foregone conclusion that even old people have peace of heart. In old age all sorts of worries rise to the surface. Possibly the hardest to overcome is the so-called unlived life. There is so much one would have liked to have and a lot that one just has not had or done. Why didn't I? Thus the questions, the fruitless questions, stab into the past.

"If I could have my life over again, I would . . ."—ah, I would commit fresh mistakes and have to leave other desires unfulfilled. For there is no life which completes everything. Actually, however, there is no such thing as an unlived life, for every life which comes from God is entire and whole. Besides, we have no claim to anything, neither beauty nor good fortune, neither wealth nor wisdom nor health. All is a gift by God's grace. To see this and bury our suppressed desires without bitterness is a task of old age.

Let us ask for the peace of Jesus Christ so that for others even in a limited way we become oases of peace.

With the ancient is wisdom; and in length of days understanding (Job 12:12).

Can we confirm that without hesitation? Scarcely, for in many cases old age has lost what gives it significance — wisdom.

Formerly — I do not mean in biblical times but about two generations ago — reverence for old age was greatly overdone. Then the pendulum swung the other way and the idolization of youth began. But anyone who seeks eternal youth — in the way our contemporaries do — cannot attain to the wisdom of age. Expressed objectively, there should be a wisdom of age, and it does exist. Almost everyone who reads these lines knows of one or more personalities whose lips in old age uttered wisdom.

But who has time now to look for wisdom, if even in advanced years he wants to take part in everything and copy youth in as much as possible? He is the loser, for to youth he appears ridiculous, and in the process he misses the precious gift of the loving, uncensorious, and appreciative wisdom of age.

Days should speak, and multitude of years should teach wisdom. But there is a spirit in man: and the inspiration of the Almighty giveth them understanding. Great men are not always wise; neither do the aged understand judgment (Job 32:7-9).

This rounds off and qualifies the last section. "Multitude of years" does not automatically bring wisdom, and it would be foolish to call anyone wise just because he is old.

"The spirit inspires us." And as the spirit bloweth where it listeth, it can inspire both young and old, even the aged, who now have leisure to hearken to the spirit, and who, if they have not lived heedlessly, understand many things better than the young. These admittedly learn little from so-called "experience," for this is something everyone has to gather for himself. Nor is every result of experience wise, for wisdom is not identical with experience. Only experience inspired by the Spirit becomes the wisdom of age, only when the "inspiration of the Almighty" gives the aged understanding are they wise. Their wisdom is effective also when it is at first rejected. Obstinacy, however, is not wisdom; "neither do the aged understand judgment."

Remember now thy Creator in the days of thy youth, while the evil days come not, nor the years draw nigh, when thou shalt say, I have no pleasure in them (Ecclesiastes 12:1).

In chapter 12 of Ecclesiastes the Bible describes most realistically the frailty of age, though in the figurative language of the Orient, which is not completely clear to us without explanation.

This first verse refers to people in the prime of life. That is the time to turn to God and be mindful of one's Creator, for when the years come of which we say, "I have no pleasure in them," it is often too late. How readily does one say when young, "I still have plenty of time. When I am old, I can think about God and religion." Who knows whether he will be old? And who knows whether when old he will still possess the mental powers to cope with the present?

From youth onward one progresses in that direction. Those who during their lifetime have attained to membership in the city of God are not so upset by the years of physical deterioration.

We must all, young and old, learn from the unadorned factuality of the Bible and not delude ourselves. Despite all the skill of science and technology we approach those years regarding which let us calmly say along with the psalmist, "We have no pleasure in them."

For honourable old age is not that which standeth in
length of time,
Nor is its measure given by number of years:
But understanding is gray hairs unto men,
And an unspotted life is ripe old age.
(Wisdom of Solomon 4:8-9, Apocrypha)

The apocryphal writings of the Old Testament, of which Luther says, "they are profitable to read," also contain frequent observations about age. Who has not already reflected that old age pure and simple, including the gray hair, is not worthy of any respect? We know old people who give us a lot of trouble and cannot arouse any respect. Our text tells us — it does not depend on years, nor on hair turned gray, but on the wisdom these years have brought and on an upright life — I might say, a life in tune with God. Above all, we must remember to ask, when we, too, are the aged and gray-haired and we often feel that youth does not offer us enough respect, "Are we wise? Are we upright?"

If we are wise, we will not be rattled by trifles and not imagine that now, in our day of all times, things are not what they used to be. Have we forgotten the way we used to think of the "old dames" when we were young ourselves? But all of us have already come across "ripe old age" and would like to attain it for ourselves.

Thou shalt rise up before the hoary head, and honour the face of the old man, and fear thy God: I am the Lord (Leviticus 19:32).

We have been discussing respect entirely from a human standpoint. Now God's peremptory words confront us — "I am the Lord." This alters the values. It is the Lord who has guided that ancient writer and us, too, all through our lives. Every time we stand for an old person, offer him our seat, show him help and respect, it is God whom we honor — not the frail, perhaps eccentric, old man, but He who has left him so long in this world and still wants him here. It is the Lord; to him alone belongs honor; before him all heads bow, gray and white ones, too. Yet God has ordained that the old are entitled to a position in this world commanding respect from the young.

One's head might reel at the thought of this, for "Not unto us, O Lord, not unto us, but unto thy name give glory," says Psalm 115 (v. 1). Remembering these words, we can better understand the honoring of age. Let us ever seek true wisdom, that we may "fear God," namely, bow at all times and places before his command. He is the Lord.

Dishonour not a man in his old age;
For some of us also are waxing old.
(Ecclesiasticus 8:6, Apocrypha)

The differences existing between the rising generation and their gradually aging parents are well known, but there is also another problem which exists when the parents are of advanced age and their family middle-aged.

It happens in old age, precisely as it did in youth — there is no mutual understanding, the "not yet" has merely changed into "no longer." There are manifold causes of misunderstanding, for which both sides are to blame.

The quotation from the book of wisdom in the Apocrypha is an exhortation to youth, which does not readily accept it, for age is to youth incomprehensible and undesired. Who thinks at twenty or thirty of being himself old and decrepit some day, and who anyway would ever want to be? One's reason tells one that it will come, but not one's feelings, and often one's feelings say, "Sooner die than be old!" Yet many who live to be old see that life can also be worthwhile then.

Can the text from Ecclesiasticus nevertheless help to promote understanding between the generations? Probably, for it makes us ponder, and pondering is the first step to possible improvement.

My son, help thy father in his old age;
And grieve him not as long as he liveth.
And if he fail in understanding, have patience with him;
And dishonour him not while thou art in thy full strength. (Ecclesiasticus 3:12-13, Apocrypha)

An old person only too often becomes vague, childish, or even irresponsible. This is frequently noticed either too soon or too late by his middle-aged family—too soon, when every difference of opinion is ascribed to "getting childish"; too late, when the lack of discernment leads to hardness and want of sympathy.

The wise man of old knew the difficulties, as the text from Ecclesiasticus shows. The family must be exhorted to take on the often heavy duty of care. The relationship is the reverse of the former one, for the family must now undertake responsibility. They find that difficult, for in a corner of their hearts they still think of their parents as the lifegivers, the one-time source of security—that is, if in their childhood they had such parents.

Old people, for their part, find it hard to be treated like children. They feel despised, no longer taken seriously, even if this is concealed by seemingly loving caresses and childish words. Better let them have what remains of their self-respect, even if this only shows as obstinacy.

With the relationship completely reversed like this the path leads downwards. That is why it is important to attain a good relationship before a final "too late" brings its own solution.

And, ye fathers, provoke not your children to wrath (Ephesians 6:4).

This thought on upbringing applies to children who are still entirely under parental authority.

But could we not apply it to parents—not only fathers but also mothers—who live with grown-up children? Do we not provoke them to resentment, to ill-humor; do we not burden them with our desires and fears and demands?

The commandment to children to honor father and mother is clear and is repeated several times in the Bible. Therefore they are not released from their duty to their parents if conversely the parents make an effort to be considerate to their children, that is, biblically expressed, not to provoke them to wrath.

Do we then provoke them to wrath? When do we do so if we are never moody? It is when we do not respect their individuality and try to treat them like little children or act as their spiritual guardian. Parents have difficulty in forgetting that the young lives were once entirely in their care. Let us therefore search ourselves, for many old people retain this attitude, especially when only one of the parents is left.

Blame for the misunderstandings between young and old is mostly attached to the young, but that is wrong. There are many failings of old age. It would do more good if old people, instead of lamenting and railing, would seek the blame first in themselves and only afterwards in others, for blame mostly exists on both sides. All sorts of things can be done to create a real community spirit, but first, wrath must be absent.

"We are free to do anything," you say. Yes, but is everything good for us? "We are free to do anything," but does everything help the building of the community? (1 Corinthians 10:23, NEB).

Nowadays the first part of this text is extremely popular — "We are free to do anything." Thus a woman getting up in years thinks, for instance, that she can vie with the young people. This is no doubt a release from the trammels of the absurd practices of earlier centuries when everything was dictated, even the very clothes one wore. But it is a bad thing if these words are taken to mean unbridled freedom. "But is everything good for us?" adds the apostle Paul.

So it is for us to distinguish what in the new freedom is good for us and our circle. In this way we place a curb on freedom. We can apply the curb ourselves, for "we are free to do anything." The words "good for us" show us our relationship to others, lay responsibility on us. It is not all the same how we behave, dress, or take part in this or that, for we are not alone in the world and are responsible for its propriety and well-being. The text emphasizes that still more in the second part where it mentions "building of the community." It is not easy to know if our conduct is helpful in this, but we must realize that it can be. Thus our freedom — if to us that means caprice and whim — is more firmly and, above all, less agreeably restricted than by an inflexible code of rules. The point about a code is that one can be sure what one must do or avoid doing, while voluntary restriction of our actions is left to ourselves.

As Christians we are not in this world to have a "nice easy" time, but to serve. Therefore we welcome joyfully the freedom that is given us, in order to use it rightly.

And when Jehu was come to Jezreel, Jezebel heard of it; and she painted her face, and tired her head, and looked out at a window (2 Kings 9:30).

In order to understand this verse properly one must know the circumstances in which the notorious Queen Jezebel is acting.

The enemy of the prophet Elisha, she is the evil spirit of her husband, King Ahab of Israel, and the city is in revolt. God's judgment on the house of Ahab has begun. But this elderly woman, mother of sons long ago grown up, thinks only of adorning and beautifying herself, no doubt in order to infatuate the leaders of the rebellion with her charms.

What message for us have these relatively unimportant words from the Bible? Do they indicate an objection to make-up? Probably not, rather a warning against wrong use of these preparations.

That concerns all of us women—especially those getting old. Certainly we should look after the body which God has given us and even adorn it, but there are limits. An elderly or old woman who is titivated so that people see she is unwilling to capitulate but is still in pursuit of conquests and effect, is a sight both embarrassing and ridiculous.

For Queen Jezebel they were the last moments of her life. She misused them shockingly. Perhaps we may spare her a thought when we — to begin with — quite innocently see our aging vision in the mirror. We cannot fix a time limit for other people, nor the manner of restriction. There are no generally valid rules for decorum in old age, but there do exist proper ideas and tact, which guide us in dressing, adorning, and turning ourselves out, and also, above all, our realization that all these superficialities must not obscure the essential!

She seeketh wool, and flax, and worketh willingly with her hands (Proverbs 31:13).

This sentence is from the description of a capable woman's life, as we find it in chapter 31 of Proverbs. Now we are no longer capable housewives, but we *can* seek wool! For this provides us with knitting, which still results in our producing useful articles to compete with factory-produced goods.

As for knitting, has it not often been a help in complicated emotional situations? The wool slips through the fingers, regularly, without interruption. I must not drop it, for one stitch has to follow the other, inexorably, consistently; one has to link with the next, without deviation, or else the work will all be spoiled, and picking up dropped stitches is laborious. Gradually the strand of wool can become the thread of life. It, too, runs through my fingers and obliges me to arrange stitch beside stitch. The one is picked up; the other taken onto the needle; there must not be any gaps, neither now in old age nor earlier when we begin to devote our thoughts to growing old.

Suppose we are feeling sad, suppose the uselessness of our aged existence is again oppressing us. Then we reach for the needles. Row after row is formed. The work grows; its purpose and shape become clear, and it becomes the symbol of constructive life.

There is fascination concealed in knitting; it is in the rhythm. Although the work often proceeds mechanically and permits our thoughts full scope, it is inexorably logical and consistent, allowing no irregularity. It firmly fixes a part of our being to the moving strand. Let us try to let the familiar process of knitting have this kind of effect on us.

Worry weighs a man down: a kind word cheers him up (Proverbs 12:25, Moffatt).

Is this not a thought for us old people? We complain so often of not being able to do anything anymore, of not even being of help to others, but we can always speak a kind word.

In the Zurich translation the text runs—"Grief in the heart of a man brings him low, a friendly word makes him glad again."

There is always a possibility of giving help thus, and there is opportunity as well. If we are at home, there is the telephone. Perhaps we know of someone who would be cheered by a friendly word—not inquisitiveness, not advice, simply some kindness of heart.

When we go out, we often sit on a seat, since our old legs won't carry us so far now. The seat is the meeting-place for old folks, even those who are strangers to each other. A friendly word forges the link. How often it brings comfort and joy!

Or news of sorrow or illness reaches us. Get paper and pen quickly; a friendly word cheers. A word of congratulation, too, rejoices the heart. All this lies within our powers. But we must not allow heaviness to settle in our own hearts. It is understandable that it finds its way in, but a good cure for that is sympathy with a fellow-creature, the kindly word for him which helps us forget our own worries.

How often are we ourselves uplifted by someone's kind word or kind deed or a sign of thoughtfulness? Let us not forget these little everyday pleasures.

Let all bitterness, and wrath, and anger, and clamour, and evil speaking, be put away from you, with all malice (Ephesians 4:31).

The malice of old age! It certainly keeps people busy! And the old people themselves? We say things like: "Well, it can't be helped." "I'm in the right." "Everybody torments me; no one bothers about me." This embitters the heart, even when "wrath" and "anger" remain far from us.

The apostle tells us "to put away all bitterness with all malice." That means that we can prevent them, and experience teaches that one should nip such things in the bud. An incipient bitterness is easy to overcome. Once it has turned into malice it becomes much harder.

In the next verse (v. 32) our text exhorts us – "And be ye kind one to another, tenderhearted."

Kindness and tenderheartedness create the spiritual climate which makes bitterness and malice impossible. For this transformation we require full concentration and the will to grasp our bitterness by the roots.

Often the offense comes from the other side. But can we not meet it with tenderheartedness? Often such offense is quite unintentional; it is due, for example, to ignorance of the state of mind of old people. So let us nip trouble in the bud, for that is easy, and "forgive one another, even as God for Christ's sake hath forgiven you."

A merry heart maketh a cheerful countenance (Proverbs 15:13).

It is not always easy to preserve a merry heart in old age. Only when we grow old and our strength begins to dwindle do we notice how much our pleasure in life, our humor and cheerfulness were due, not as we proudly imagined, to a higher moral level, but to a youthful physique.

So we must learn cheerfulness afresh when old, for a happy old person, sympathetic to others, can be a blessing to all around.

But how does one learn cheerfulness? Maybe by taking careful note. The old can enjoy and appreciate times when things go well, better than the young, for they have recognized the value of things familiar, unimportant and transitory, in spite of all they have had to forego.

We become happier once we have learned to get over pinpricks and attach no importance to them. This really can be learned, certainly not overnight, but in time. How? By not taking oneself so seriously! It is not easy, but it is worthwhile. "A merry heart maketh a cheerful countenance." Thus cheerfulness becomes visible, and it is infectious.

DEATH STANDS ABOVE ME

Death stands above me, whispering low
I know not what into my ear:
Of his strange language all I know
Is, there is not a word of fear.

Walter Savage Landor

FINIS

I strove with none, for none was worth my strife,
Nature I loved and, next to Nature, Art:
I warmed both hands before the fire of life;
It sinks, and I am ready to depart.

Walter Savage Landor

North winds bring rain: slander brings angry looks (Proverbs 25:23, Moffatt).

Instead of a happy face a scowling, alas, even an ill-natured one, is often seen.

What causes the ill nature of old age? Is there such a thing? Let us see if we can detect it in old women's faces. We are horrified! Certainly there are cheerful, pleasant, and therefore beautiful, faces, but there are others, too. In old men the apathy of age predominates, in women, unfortunately a malicious tendency to gossip and give uncharitable criticism, "slander," as our text calls it.

When we look into our own hearts, we are still more horrified at this evil, bitter, provoked thing which often thrusts itself from lowest depths to the surface. What is the cause of it? Is the ill nature of old age different from that of earlier years? Scarcely, but one is perpetually haunted by the words "too late." And old people generally have plenty of time to brood over all their stirred-up thoughts, all their real and imagined slights. Does an unlived life reveal itself in grudges? Is the more and more burdensome everyday jog-trot to blame? Or is it reaction to the gentle but perpetual brushing-off, a seeking to get back by extremely tyrannical bossiness or constant criticizing? We try to get to the root of the trouble, to expose and recognize it, if possible to render it harmless by ridiculing it. This is not easy but necessary. We want to see in others not cross but happy faces and in ourselves a heart full of gladness, for all ill nature causes hurt.

... but in humility count others better than yourselves. Let each of you look not only to his own interests, but also to the interests of others (Philippians 2:3-4, RSV) .

Tactful everyday behavior, for example, when sharing a home with younger people, is not easy to achieve. When should one join in, withdraw, give the benefit of one's experience, when listen and be silent? There are no rules of conduct but one, which is part of the self-discipline of old age — whether one goes or stays, speaks or remains silent, one must do it without ulterior thoughts, that is, with thoughts *"also* to the interests of others."

Ulterior thoughts may be criticism suppressed or secretly indulged, and the abominable feeling of being slighted, which can embitter life so much. Moreover, the exhortation is "in humility count others better than yourselves" — a difficult undertaking, not only in old age, but particularly then, if after a long life one fancies that one is "wise" and "superior."

However, our difficult text casts a shaft of light on two plain little words — "only" and "also." Not "only" looking to his own interests. Thus one is automatically assured of looking also to his own interests. *"Also* to the interests of others." This "also" points back to what is our own. The text demands reciprocal action between others and ourselves, neither complete self-renunciation, nor pure sacrifice, nor selfish brooding on our hurt feelings and our demands, which can oppress young people so heavily.

When I sit in darkness, the Lord shall be a light unto me (Micah 7:8).

Only those who have been through it know! The great darkness which threatens us is death. There are times when it envelops us, for the thought of it has stealthily invaded our conscious mind, e.g., through threatening illness, and penetrated to our subconscious, bidding fair to have complete mastery over us. Any physical discomfort intensifies it enormously. It falls like a veil over the loveliest sunshine, over everything good and fine on earth. We know that the shadow of death will finally close our eyes, and we do not perceive the light of God until a moment comes during prayer or Bible reading when a text suddenly lights up and seems to be written for us personally, flashing like lightning right in our everyday lives — "The Lord is my light."

Notwithstanding, I still sit in darkness; the physical discomfort has not been relieved; the fear of death persists. But it has changed. The light of the Lord illumines us, that light which knows no darkness.

I am the darkness; the Lord is the light. But the light comes to me, a personal approach, like the text which stirred me. And I know — "When I sit in darkness, the Lord shall be a light unto me."

O Lord, I know that the way of man is not in himself: it is not in man that walketh to direct his steps (Jeremiah 10:23).

From our earliest days it is our desire and aim to direct our own steps. The prophet's words show us the true facts of the case. It is God who guides our steps and leads us from childhood to youth, from youth to maturity, and finally to old age. We would fain retard or hasten our pace, for we imagine we are masters over our own lives.

In youth one presses forward. One would like to be grown up, in the midst of life; one reaches out, refuses to linger or wait for one's maturity. One's steps are nevertheless guided onwards, and the wayfarer enters upon new paths of life.

Stop! We don't like them! We're going too fast! Our mirror shows us our new face, our aging appearance. Our steps are being checked and directed as we do not wish. No, no, not that!

What remedies do we then seek? The paintpot and brush, self-mortification and diet, just to avoid the appointed path? Because we want to direct our paths ourselves, we direct ourselves to our misfortune.

"I know," says the prophet, "that it is not in the power of man to determine his ways"—nor the time when we are to tread this or that path.

Let us readily yield to that hand which guides the wayfarer's step and determines a man's ways.

Yea, though I walk through the valley of the shadow of death, I will fear no evil: for thou art with me; thy rod and thy staff they comfort me (Psalm 23:4).

When old we often walk through the valley of the shadow, through hours of remorse, fear, pain. We cannot honestly say with the psalmist, "I will fear no evil." For just this is our great weakness — to fear evil. Wakeful night hours especially are full of such forebodings, and the fear of death can take hold of us heavily.

Let us not deny these hours; they, too, are part of our life. Nevertheless we look for a solution, for help; for something within us knows that this spiritual state is a weakness. Our text helps us, as does the whole Twenty-third Psalm, which is so short that we can learn it by heart in spite of our aged memory. Above all, the words "for *thou* art with me" comfort us. We cling to this "thou," for it means the removal of our troubles. Admittedly it does not work like magic, for behind the "thou" stand not our foolish imaginings and not only our beliefs but the living Person of Jesus Christ. That is why peace and quietness cannot be gained by force. One must wait till they are given.

O give thanks unto the Lord; for he is good: for his mercy endureth for ever (Psalm 136:1).

Yes, give thanks! Perhaps we use this verse or a similar one as grace before meat. But experience shows that we have never quite mastered thanksgiving. Now in old age thanksgiving is far from our thoughts. Why? Because we have so much to complain about! We do sometimes give thanks — perhaps for the gift of one more day. But do we always? Is this new day not full of petty annoyances, pain, discomfort? And if we encounter something pleasant, do we give thanks? Or do we yield ourselves up completely to the pleasure? Yes, we ought to learn thanksgiving, we older people particularly. Begin with the new day, go on systematically with all the good things we enjoy — a bed, a roof over our heads, a kind friend, a picture we like, our Bible lying open, the flowers we were given, or a letter, a visit, a smile, a kindly act. In short, be thankful for everything which comes our way. We shall see how our life is brightened by thanksgiving.

If perhaps in a sleepless night fear lays hold on us — fear of the future, a possible accident, pain, or death — let us try thanksgiving! Then the billows sink; then we see that what we feared is not inevitable (except death, which no one escapes), that there is so much around us worthy of rejoicing.

God is near. We give him thanks and in time perhaps learn the hardest lesson — to give thanks for what troubles and hurts, even when we cannot see why the hardship has befallen us.

The Lord hath need of them (Matthew 21:3).

It is a she-ass which the Lord required for his entry into Jerusalem. I, too, would like to be one of whom Jesus says, "The Lord hath need of her." Perhaps there is some task which I, too, could do for him?

The demand "The Lord hath need of them" and the readiness of the owner to accede to it have always moved me.

But is the comparison of the ass, for example, with me correct? The ass has no idea that she is required. She merely obeys the behest of her master. And who will command me, if I would fain be the ass? Do the image and my desire not coincide? Am I always my own master? Do I not belong to many earthly masters? Are there not many people and things which hold me fast? One time it is my husband, another the children or the housekeeping, my social obligations, property, affairs, or occupation. If the Lord really says, "I have need of thee," shall I be set free? Shall I really free myself for the task?

And now that I am old? Is there still a task, is it perhaps now within me, in my forced separation from affairs and surroundings, from life and activity? Be that as it may — I would like to be that ass! The call does not come to everyone. There were plenty of asses in Jerusalem then, and the Lord knew the one and called her. That is the one I would like to be!

Let us open our ears to hear when the Lord calls us in one way or another and seeks to use our feeble strength!

Yet a little sleep, a little slumber, a little folding of the hands to sleep: So shall thy poverty come as one that travelleth; and thy want as an armed man (Proverbs 24:33-34).

Does this apply to us old people? The second part certainly does not literally, for our doings generally no longer increase our means and our indolence seldom makes us poorer.

But in other ways it has a definite message for us. How loath we are to get up in the morning; with what reluctance we leave the comfortable armchair; how often do we neglect to tidy up, to make the house look nicer, or to do a bit of necessary cleaning, which we very well could do! And the results? Have we never come across an old person's fusty neglected home? Think of the unwritten letters, the unfinished jobs, the kindly acts given up, and the slackening attitude—"What's the use? It's not worthwhile bothering now." "Yet a little sleep, yet a little slumber"—when one knows perfectly well that one can get up and still has quite enough strength to maintain a certain discipline.

That's it—discipline! As long as ever possible—for the time comes when it no longer is, when we are entirely dependent on the help of others—let us strive to keep a grip on ourselves and carry out our little duties, without burdening others. For our powers are feeble, our ability to do things wanes, it is the way of the world. But it is worthwhile always to do the job that is nearest, however enticing we may find it "to fold the hands to sleep."

If you will throw your treasures to the ground,
and fling your gold of Ophir in the stream,
and make the Almighty himself your treasure,
sound wisdom your wealth,
then the Almighty shall be a joy to you,
and you can raise your eyes to God.
(Job 22:24-26, Moffatt)

What a fine poetic text describing the renunciation of worldly wealth—gold in the dust and in the brook, no longer hoarded and guarded, all surrendered to God! God is to take the place of gold and his laws replace silver. What does that mean translated into our language? This means the yielding of our possessions up to God. Jesus, too, repeatedly teaches this in the New Testament.

We find it hard! What? Are we to throw away, to squander our gold, i.e., our means? No, we can't do it. Our whole being resists the thought. We have been much too solidly brought up for that. In the Book of Job, too, the passage is only an illustration. What is demanded is not squandering but shifting of emphasis, from ourselves as sole controllers of our means over to God, the real controller of them. "The silver is mine and the gold is mine," says God through the prophet Haggai, and it is for us to strive to keep this constantly before us.

The thought is not agreeable but salutary and draws us away from the petty possessiveness so natural to us. Let us not deceive ourselves! We are very far from placing our possessions in God's hands.

The reward which our text promises is delight in

the Almighty. What are our earthly goods in comparison, although, as we cannot deny, they also provide us with delight in life? But God demands control over them, even if we certainly shall not throw our gold and our riches to the ground or in the water, but utilize them soundly.

. . . *neither be ye sorry; for the joy of the Lord is your strength* (Nehemiah 8:10) .

In old age joy displays itself outwardly much less. This is well known. One only needs to look at old people's faces and listen to their talk, the lamentations and the grumbles, to be convinced of that. Is this grumbling justified? We can answer that question both with yes and with no. With yes, for old age in itself is certainly no delight and all the woes are not easy to bear. But at the same time we can answer no, for a large part of the grumbling is unnecessary. It springs from egotism and self-pity desiring to air itself, seeking to intensify itself through the commiseration of the listener. The woes are not relieved by this, but rather aggravated. Our text shows us the way out of the perpetual lamentations, away from ourselves. Let us seek joy where it is to be found — in the Lord. This word was spoken to the people of Israel when they were in a far from enviable situation, surrounded by enemies, engaged in rebuilding their ruined home, after the recognition of their own guilt, which consisted in having departed from God and his law.

But God permitted them joy, joy in the Lord, which could express itself in outward pleasures, for example, in eating. There was only one condition attached: this joy must be shared. No one was to eat his fill if his neighbor were hungry.

Down the centuries this text comes to us all: joy as a refuge precisely when we are in a situation we do not like and would fain escape from, joy as strength — both translations are possible — when the humdrum life of old age makes us weak and slack.

If we observe this command, we shall leave off lamenting, abandon our touchy self-centered outlook, and joy will light up even an aged and infirm life.

Come, then, stiffen your drooping arms and shaking knees, and keep your steps from wavering. Then the disabled limb will not be put out of joint, but regain its former powers (Hebrews 12:12-13, NEB) .

Here the writer of the epistle to the Hebrews quotes the Old Testament, a text from Isaiah and one from Proverbs, to encourage the brethren and lead them in God's paths.

If we have difficulty in walking and all efforts to

cure this fail, these words may perhaps hurt us deeply. But why? To a certain extent this challenge is also outwardly helpful. Do something! Don't let yourselves go; be willing to try stiffening your arms and knees! To be sure, there is a physical limit; we can only go so far. But inwardly and spiritually this admonition is much more applicable. It seeks to activate us and make us ready for service, for thus even old people are worthwhile companions when they try, in spite of crippled legs, to walk in the straight paths of the Lord. Our path on earth leads through suffering to the grave, but the straight paths to which the Lord calls us lead to eternity.

O Lord, thou hast searched me, and known me. Thou knowest my downsitting and mine uprising, thou understandest my thought afar off (Psalm 139:1-2).

The omnipresence of God is something beyond comprehension. The psalmist says in the following verses of Psalm 139, "Such knowledge is too wonderful for me; it is high, I cannot attain unto it." But it *can* be experienced.

This knowledge can oppress a man; it can pursue him. But why should it? Do we not suffer in old age particularly from loneliness? Do we not complain of being neglected? Yet our psalm tells us we are never alone but are cheered by a loving Presence. Nothing can happen to us unknown to God.

Does that mean that in the earthly sphere of our existence we are under special protection? Experience proves it otherwise, for God the Father, who sent his own Son into severest suffering, also requires much from his earthly children.

Nevertheless, and precisely when things are going the way we don't like, we know that the Lord is near. This psalm describes it further: "Thou compassest my path and my lying down."

What comfort for the old, the sick, and the bedridden, what deliverance from solitude! Such intimate companionship, even when accompanied by great love, is not possible with another human being.

Why are we so slow to see this? Because we fear judgment! Could we not rather feel the loving hand of the Father, who "understands my thought afar off"?

Then we would be relieved of our loneliness, even if because of our human frailty we did not always admit it.

A time to get, and a time to lose; a time to keep, and a time to cast away (Ecclesiastes 3:6).

This is a suitable text for old age. For "casting away" has to be learned, and above all the realization must come that one will have to part, for example, with one's belongings, since everything has "its time." In old age the obvious meaninglessness of earthly existence is often made clear to us. How attached we have been to this or that; how vitally important to us were all sorts of things! Ecclesiastes, from which our text is taken, says of various things that they are "vanity and vexation of spirit," namely futile, or as Luther translates it, "All is vanity."

Is that the case with us? Happy are we if we recognize the vanity in good time, and the parting no longer hurts! For, after all, one has loved everything that made up one's life, and that is right. Recognition of vanity should not lead to sorrow or indifference, but should mean a correct allocation of values.

Too great indifference leads to egotism. Other people, for example, young folk, are at the stage of searching, building, retaining. Let us not forget that, and let us not expect them to understand fully our process of "losing" and "casting away."

The Preacher speaks wisely—"To every thing there is a season, and a time to every purpose under the heaven." The art of living consists in realizing the right time and its demands and acting accordingly. Happy are the old who recognize this their season and live it to the full!

But man dieth, and wasteth away: yea, man giveth up the ghost, and where is he? (Job 14:10).

These are the words of an Old Testament speaker—that means someone who knew nothing of Christ's resurrection. But we, too, are familiar with this query. It is in the mind of every natural person. For death is the great mystery, something inevitably impending, even if we often forget it, or try to.

Is one to ponder upon death? That is done, certainly. But does it not stand before us like a black wall?

I do not know whether there is, humanly speaking, an effective preparation for death. For how is one to prepare for something one cannot know? And where are we after death? Our text, too, asks this.

Death is not a friend; on the contrary, it is the last enemy, as the Bible calls it. At any rate, running away from it is definitely wrong. Death is the certain end of our earthly life. Its personification, often presented in the intellectual and artistic history of mankind, is also wrong. This robs it of some of its mystery.

We must face it boldly, following the example of Jesus.

Why seek ye the living among the dead? He is not here, but is risen (Luke 24:5-6).

The New Testament does not say much about life after death, but enough to enable us to look toward our own death with hope.

Does our present life perhaps acquire more value and color through thoughts of death? Yes, every event, every phase of life, every encounter has its end. Daily experiences show that. And death is the greatest, the most inexorable end.

Because I clearly understand about the course of life steadily proceeding toward its end I am not so terrified — even if it is painful — of leaving the world, my accustomed surroundings, beloved friends. How much have I not already left behind? What is now left in me of my childhood? At most perhaps a few threads of vague recollection. What I dread is the last step, leaving the visible self which can establish contact with others.

But behind the portals is my Lord, who is life, and I believe in him and his resurrection.

. . . *Christ in you, the hope of glory* (Colossians 1:27) .

If Christ is in us, he is so today, now, at this moment, tomorrow, the day after, and until the last day of our earthly life, not only in the life to come. If he is in us, he transfigures the present, helps us to fulfill the task which is laid upon each one according to his circumstances and estate. It is precisely through the presence of Christ that the present acquires its highest value, and our activities, which seem so ordinary to us, their importance.

The text, however, does not stop at the present; it speaks of the hope of glory, and where there is hope there is also a future. Glory is not to be found anywhere on this earth, because the way of all things here is rising and passing away. So the text from Colossians opens for us a clear view of eternal life.

We need not try to imagine it. All the more can we hold fast to it — Christ and glory! So we have a future based on the past, that is, on the life of Jesus, his death and resurrection, a future to be grasped in the present, shining into all eternity.